JAZZ PLAY ALONG

Book and CD for B♭, E♭ and C Instruments

Wayne Shorter

10 WAYNE SHORTER CLASSICS

Arranged and Produced by Mark Taylor

BOOK

CD

ISBN 978-0-634-06192-9

HAL•LEONARD®

7777 W. BLUEMOUND RD. P.O. BOX 13819 MILWAUKEE, WI 53213

Visit Hal Leonard Online at
www.halleonard.com

Wayne Shorter

Arranged and Produced by
Mark Taylor

Featured Players:

Graham Breedlove-Trumpet
John Desalme-Tenor Sax
Tony Nalker-Piano
Jim Roberts-Bass
Steve Fidyk-Drums

Recorded at Bias Studios, Springfield, Virginia
Bob Dawson, Engineer

HOW TO USE THE CD:

Each song has <u>two</u> tracks:

1) Split Track/Melody

Woodwind, Brass, Keyboard, and **Mallet Players** can use this track as a learning tool for melody, style and inflection.

Bass Players can learn and perform with this track – remove the recorded bass track by turning down the volume on the LEFT channel.

Keyboard and **Guitar Players** can learn and perform with this track – remove the recorded piano part by turning down the volume on the RIGHT channel.

2) Full Stereo Track

Soloists or **Groups** can learn and perform with this accompaniment track with the RHYTHM SECTION only.

CHILDREN OF THE NIGHT

MUSIC BY WAYNE SHORTER

E.S.P.

C VERSION

MUSIC BY WAYNE SHORTER

FOOTPRINTS

C VERSION

BY WAYNE SHORTER

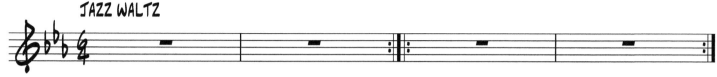

JUJU

C VERSION

MUSIC BY WAYNE SHORTER

NEFERTITI

CD
9: SPLIT TRACK/MELODY
10: FULL STEREO TRACK

C VERSION MEDIUM SWING

BY WAYNE SHORTER

MAHJONG

CD

⓫ : SPLIT TRACK/MELODY
⓬ : FULL STEREO TRACK

C VERSION

MUSIC BY WAYNE SHORTER

SOLOS (2 X'S)

Fmi11   Eb6/9   Fmi11   Eb6/9

Fmi11   Eb6/9   Fmi11   Eb6/9

Dbma9   Eb6/9   Dbma9   Eb6/9

Dbma9   Eb6/9   Dbma9   Eb6/9

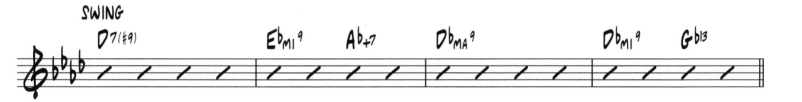

SWING

D7(#9)   Ebmi9   Ab+7   Dbma9   Dbmi9   Gb13

AFRO

Fmi11   Eb6/9   Fmi11   Eb6/9

Fmi11   Eb6/9   Fmi11   Eb6/9   D.S. AL CODA LAST TIME

CODA

Fmi11   Eb6/9   Eb6/9/Db

NIGHT DREAMER

C VERSION

MUSIC BY WAYNE SHORTER

WITCH HUNT

CD
◆15: SPLIT TRACK/MELODY
◆16: FULL STEREO TRACK

C VERSION   MEDIUM SWING   MUSIC BY WAYNE SHORTER

CD

SPEAK NO EVIL

C VERSION

MUSIC BY WAYNE SHORTER

SOLOS (ONE CHORUS ONLY)

D.S. AL CODA

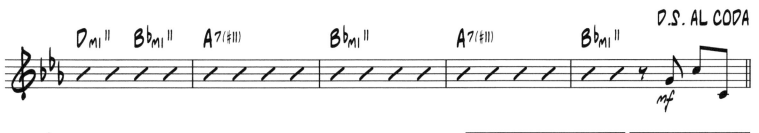

PLAY FIRST TIME ONLY

YES AND NO

C VERSION

MUSIC BY WAYNE SHORTER

* SOLOS
D13SUS

Dma9   Ami7   D7

Gma7 F7 Bbma7   Emi7

Ami7(b5)   D7(b9)   Gmi7

(Gmi7)   C13   Fmi9

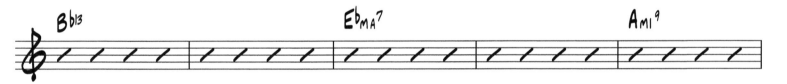

Bb13   Ebma7   Ami9

(Ami9)   D13SUS

Dma9   Ami7   D7

Gma7 F7 Bbma7   Emi7   D.S. AL CODA

CODA
(Bbma7)   Emi11

(BACK TO * FOR MORE SOLOS)

CHILDREN OF THE NIGHT

MUSIC BY WAYNE SHORTER

TO CODA ⊕

SOLOS (ONE CHORUS ONLY)

D.S. AL CODA

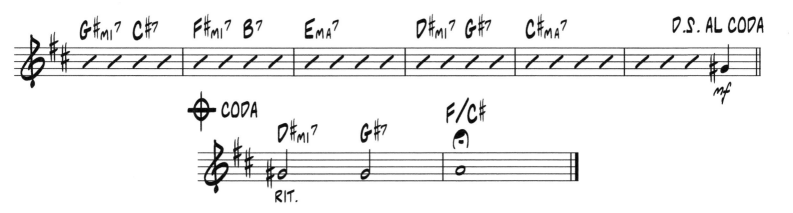

⊕ CODA

RIT.

20

FOOTPRINTS

By Wayne Shorter

B♭ Version

JUJU

MUSIC BY WAYNE SHORTER

NEFERTITI

CD
◆9: SPLIT TRACK/MELODY
◆10: FULL STEREO TRACK

Bb VERSION

MEDIUM SWING

BY WAYNE SHORTER

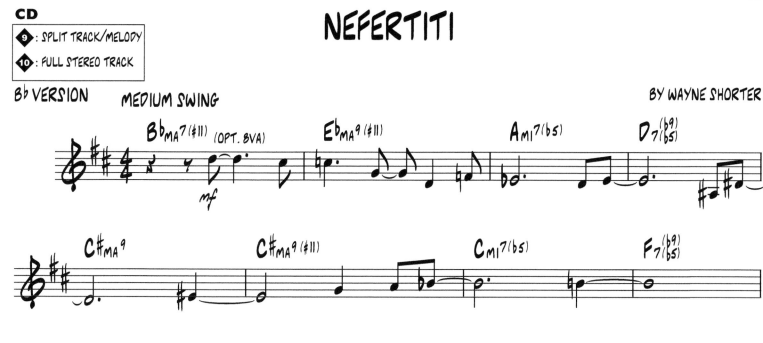

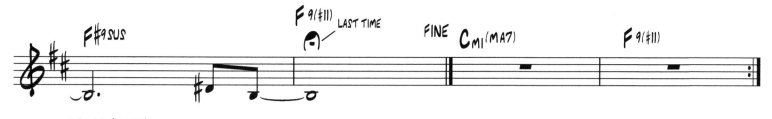

CD

11 : SPLIT TRACK/MELODY
12 : FULL STEREO TRACK

MAHJONG

Bb VERSION

MUSIC BY WAYNE SHORTER

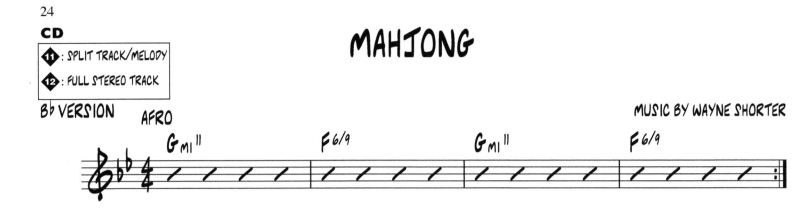

SOLOS (2 X'S)

SWING

AFRO

D.S. AL CODA
LAST TIME

CODA

NIGHT DREAMER

B♭ VERSION

MUSIC BY WAYNE SHORTER

WITCH HUNT

Bb VERSION   MEDIUM SWING

MUSIC BY WAYNE SHORTER

SPEAK NO EVIL

SOLOS (ONE CHORUS ONLY)

D.S. AL CODA

CODA

PLAY FIRST TIME ONLY

YES AND NO

B♭ VERSION

MUSIC BY WAYNE SHORTER

✱ SOLOS
E¹³SUS

EMA⁹
                                                        BMI⁷   E⁷

AMA⁷   G⁷   CMA⁷
                                    F#MI⁷

BMI⁷⁽♭5⁾
                        E⁷⁽♭9⁾   AMI⁷

(AMI⁷)   D¹³   GMI⁹

C¹³   FMA⁷   BMI⁹

(BMI⁹)   E¹³SUS

EMA⁹
                                                        BMI⁷   E⁷

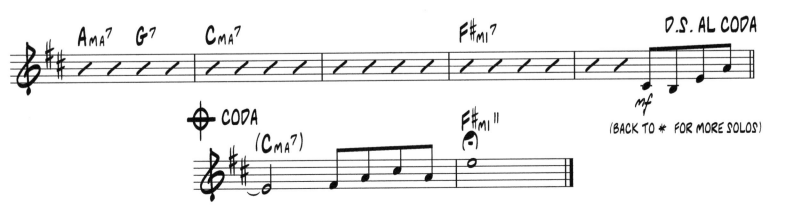
AMA⁷   G⁷   CMA⁷
                                    F#MI⁷   D.S. AL CODA

mf
(BACK TO ✱ FOR MORE SOLOS)

⊕ CODA
(CMA⁷)   F#MI¹¹

CHILDREN OF THE NIGHT

Eb VERSION   SWING

MUSIC BY WAYNE SHORTER

CD

E.S.P.

E♭ VERSION

FAST SWING

MUSIC BY WAYNE SHORTER

FOOTPRINTS

BY WAYNE SHORTER

E♭ VERSION

JUJU

Eb VERSION

MUSIC BY WAYNE SHORTER

NEFERTITI

CD
9: SPLIT TRACK/MELODY
10: FULL STEREO TRACK

Eb VERSION

BY WAYNE SHORTER

MEDIUM SWING

SOLOS (2 X'S)

Mahjong

Eb VERSION

MUSIC BY WAYNE SHORTER

SOLOS (2 X'S)

Dmi11 | C6/9 | Dmi11 | C6/9

Dmi11 | C6/9 | Dmi11 | C6/9

Bbma9 | C6/9 | Bbma9 | C6/9

Bbma9 | C6/9 | Bbma9 | C6/9

SWING

B7(#9) | Cmi9   F+7 | Bbma9 | Bbmi9   Eb13

AFRO

Dmi11 | C6/9 | Dmi11 | C6/9

D.S. AL CODA
LAST TIME

Dmi11 | C6/9 | Dmi11 | C6/9

CODA

C6/9/Bb

Dmi11 | C6/9

NIGHT DREAMER

WITCH HUNT

CD
15: SPLIT TRACK/MELODY
16: FULL STEREO TRACK

Eb VERSION MEDIUM SWING

MUSIC BY WAYNE SHORTER

CD

⬥ 17 : SPLIT TRACK/MELODY
⬥ 18 : FULL STEREO TRACK

SPEAK NO EVIL

E♭ VERSION

MUSIC BY WAYNE SHORTER

SOLOS (ONE CHORUS ONLY)

D.S. AL CODA

CODA

PLAY FIRST TIME ONLY

YES AND NO

Eb VERSION

MUSIC BY WAYNE SHORTER

✱ SOLOS

B¹³ˢᵁˢ

Bᴍᴀ⁹   F#ᴍɪ⁷   B⁷

Eᴍᴀ⁷   D⁷   Gᴍᴀ⁷   C#ᴍɪ⁷

F#ᴍɪ⁷⁽ᵇ⁵⁾   B⁷⁽ᵇ⁹⁾   Eᴍɪ⁷

(Eᴍɪ⁷)   A¹³   Dᴍɪ⁹

G¹³   Cᴍᴀ⁷   F#ᴍɪ⁹

(F#ᴍɪ⁹)   B¹³ˢᵁˢ

Bᴍᴀ⁹   F#ᴍɪ⁷   B⁷

D.S. AL CODA

Eᴍᴀ⁷   D⁷   Gᴍᴀ⁷   C#ᴍɪ⁷

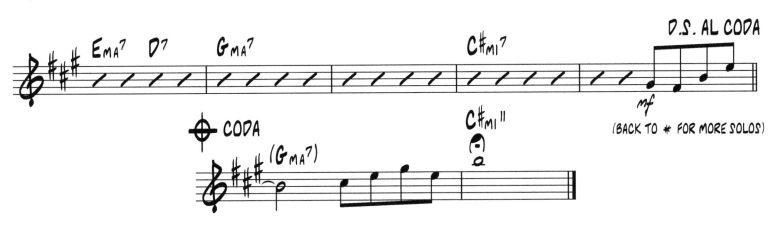

⊕ CODA

(Gᴍᴀ⁷)   C#ᴍɪ¹¹

mf

(BACK TO ✱ FOR MORE SOLOS)

CHILDREN OF THE NIGHT

MUSIC BY WAYNE SHORTER

CD
- **1**: SPLIT TRACK/MELODY
- **2**: FULL STEREO TRACK

: C VERSION

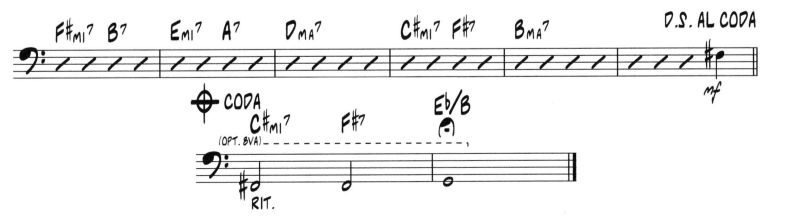

E.S.P.

𝄢: C VERSION

MUSIC BY WAYNE SHORTER

FOOTPRINTS

BY WAYNE SHORTER

𝄢: C VERSION

JUJU

MUSIC BY WAYNE SHORTER

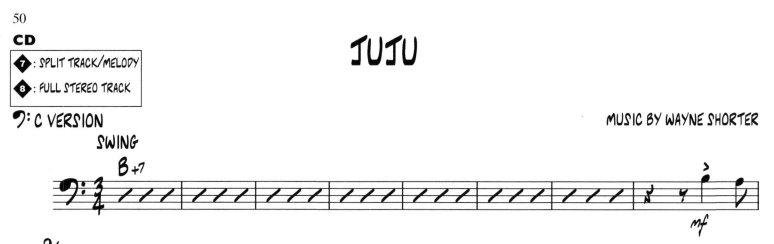

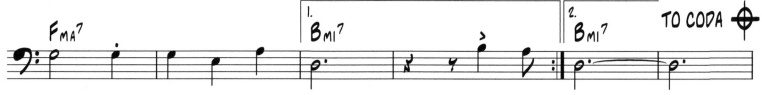

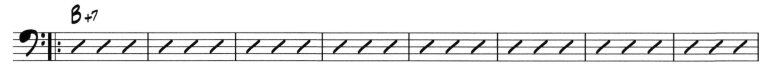

NEFERTITI

BY WAYNE SHORTER

CD
9 : SPLIT TRACK/MELODY
10 : FULL STEREO TRACK

𝄢: C VERSION

MEDIUM SWING

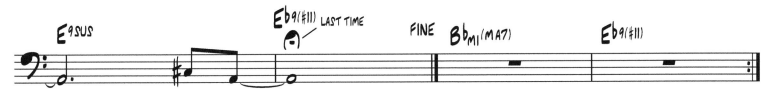

SOLOS (2 X'S)

CD
11 : SPLIT TRACK/MELODY
12 : FULL STEREO TRACK

MAHJONG

MUSIC BY WAYNE SHORTER

𝄢: C VERSION AFRO

TO CODA ⊕

SOLOS (2 X'S)

Fmi¹¹   Eb6/9   Fmi¹¹   Eb6/9

Fmi¹¹   Eb6/9   Fmi¹¹   Eb6/9

Dbma⁹   Eb6/9   Dbma⁹   Eb6/9

Dbma⁹   Eb6/9   Dbma⁹   Eb6/9

SWING

D7(#9)   Ebmi⁹   Ab+7   Dbma⁹   Dbmi⁹   Gb13

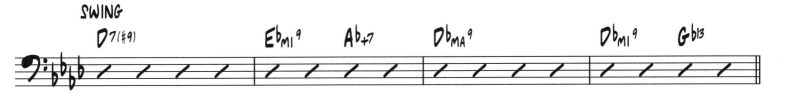

AFRO

Fmi¹¹   Eb6/9   Fmi¹¹   Eb6/9

D.S. AL CODA
LAST TIME

Fmi¹¹   Eb6/9   Fmi¹¹   Eb6/9

CODA

Fmi¹¹   Eb6/9   Eb6/9/Db

NIGHT DREAMER

𝄢: C VERSION

MUSIC BY WAYNE SHORTER

WITCH HUNT

MUSIC BY WAYNE SHORTER

CD
⑮ : SPLIT TRACK/MELODY
⑯ : FULL STEREO TRACK

SPEAK NO EVIL

MUSIC BY WAYNE SHORTER

CD

17 : SPLIT TRACK/MELODY
18 : FULL STEREO TRACK

♪: C VERSION   MEDIUM SWING

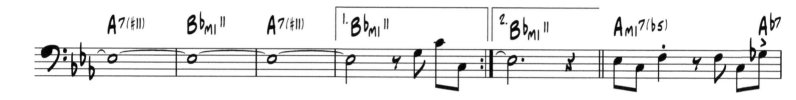

SOLOS (ONE CHORUS ONLY)

D.S. AL CODA

PLAY FIRST TIME ONLY

CD
⟨19⟩ : SPLIT TRACK/MELODY
⟨20⟩ : FULL STEREO TRACK

♪: C VERSION

YES AND NO

MUSIC BY WAYNE SHORTER

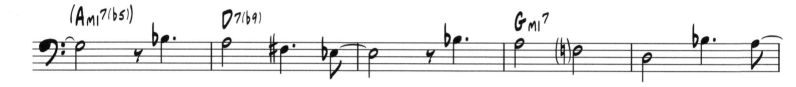

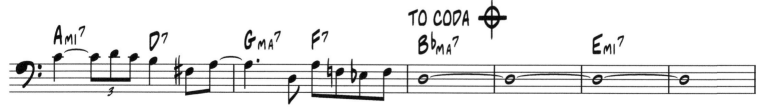

✱ SOLOS

D13SUS

Dma9 ... Ami7 D7

Gma7 F7 Bbma7 ... Emi7

Ami7(b5) ... D7(b9) ... Gmi7

(Gmi7) ... C13 ... Fmi9

Bb13 ... Ebma7 ... Ami9

(Ami9) ... D13SUS

Dma9 ... Ami7 D7

D.S. AL CODA

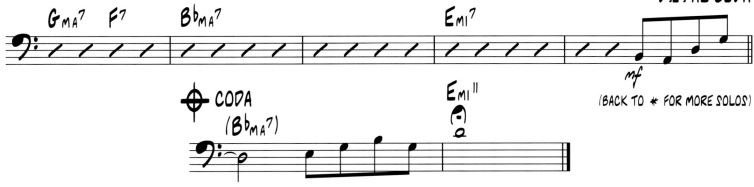
Gma7 F7 Bbma7 ... Emi7

mf
(BACK TO ✱ FOR MORE SOLOS)

⊕ CODA
(Bbma7) ... Emi11